THE CAMBRIDGE MISCELLANY

XVI

THE STUDY OF DRAMA

T0346118

THE STUDY OF DRAMA

BY

HARLEY GRANVILLE-BARKER

*A Lecture given at Cambridge
on 2 August 1934, with notes
subsequently added*

CAMBRIDGE
AT THE UNIVERSITY PRESS
1934

CAMBRIDGE UNIVERSITY PRESS
Cambridge, New York, Melbourne, Madrid, Cape Town,
Singapore, São Paulo, Delhi, Tokyo, Mexico City

Cambridge University Press
The Edinburgh Building, Cambridge CB2 8RU, UK

Published in the United States of America by Cambridge University Press, New York

www.cambridge.org
Information on this title: www.cambridge.org/9781107665590

© Cambridge University Press 1934

This publication is in copyright. Subject to statutory exception
and to the provisions of relevant collective licensing agreements,
no reproduction of any part may take place without the written
permission of Cambridge University Press.

First published 1934
First paperback edition 2011

A catalogue record for this publication is available from the British Library

ISBN 978-1-107-66559-0 Paperback

Cambridge University Press has no responsibility for the persistence or
accuracy of URLs for external or third-party internet websites referred to in
this publication, and does not guarantee that any content on such websites is,
or will remain, accurate or appropriate.

CONTENTS

THE STUDY OF DRAMA

A SUMMER MEETING in the University of Cambridge devoted to Masterpieces of Drama and the Modern Theatre; that, surely, is something of a landmark in the history of the drama in England! Only very recently can such a thing have become possible. Masterpieces of Dramatic *Literature* we might have had. But drama as drama, considered in relation to the theatre—and to the *modern* theatre; lectures upon the repertory system, upon experiments in staging, even upon the ballet, and, as an integral part of the programme, performances of plays by members of the University (but not, unhappily, ballets!)—forty, thirty, ten years ago, could such a thing have been? In addition, there are classes for amateur producers of plays. And—is not this a happy symbol of the reconciling of University and Theatre?—the lady who directs them has, besides her own pre-eminent claim upon the occasion, another and very glamorous one in the eyes of many of us: she is Ellen Terry's daughter.

This reconciliation has not been easily achieved. For two hundred years and more the drama, except as it belonged to book learning, was effectively banished from both Universities. In Oxford, not till late in the nineteenth century could professional companies act in term time, and not until 1884 were undergraduates allowed to act. In Cambridge, from about 1830 onwards, occasional semi-private performances by undergraduates, and after a while the existence of an amateur club, were tolerated by the authorities. The Cambridge undergraduate was possibly more unruly than his Oxford brother. Possibly the authorities held that, though his time might be better employed, it didn't follow (if they forbad him to act) that it *would* be. But till 1894 the Vice-Chancellor had absolute power to forbid all professional performances in Cambridge; and for long—in term time at least—he exercised it (A).

For some years before, however, a more liberal opinion had been developing; and among the leaders of it was a man of character. He not only had liberal opinions, in this as in other matters, but he had the courage of them. And when, after many difficulties, the Vice-Chancellor was deprived of the more drastic of his powers and it was worth while to build a reasonably well-equipped theatre—the present New Theatre—J. W. Clark, Fellow of Trinity and Registrary of the University, joined the Board of its Directors, and till his death in 1910 did all he could to help it. (He was also, by the way, an authority upon the topography and architecture of the University, and it is his little guide that—if you are a stranger here—the programme recommends you to buy.) It must have been just about 1895, when the New Theatre was really new, that I paid my own first visit to Cambridge. I cannot remember in the least what brought me. But, oddly enough, I can vividly recall walking down the long concrete passage that leads one out of the theatre, and seeing in front of me a burly, bearded, springily stepping man. That, I was told, was J. W. Clark, on whom the whole fortune of the drama in Cambridge depended. And this, I think, was really true. He had been chiefly responsible for the famous series of Greek plays given in the 1880's (Parry's and Stanford's music remains as testimony to the quality of the productions). He encouraged the A.D.C. He must have steered it, as he helped steer the New Theatre, through many difficulties. He must, in fact, have done more than anyone of his day to restore the credit of the living drama in the University. For he had an uncovenanted and uncalculating love of the theatre. I don't suppose that all its modern manifestations would have appealed to him. But his opposition was, it seems, almost as stimulating as his support. He had in himself, in fact, that greatest of dramatic virtues, a generous vitality. In blessing or damning he would certainly have been the liveliest of figures at this present meeting. And as I feel that, to some extent, I owe him my own good fortune in being here to-night, perhaps—even though I was a stranger to him and am not much better than a stranger to Cambridge—I may be allowed to begin by commemorating his name.

If we go back a little further—to the sixteenth century, which *is* but a little further in the

4

University's history—we find drama, of a kind, very much alive in Cambridge. Not only in those days were members of the University permitted to act, they were by various College statutes directly enjoined to, and fined if they did not. Trinity, for instance, by the statutes of 1560, had to produce five plays a year.[1] But this was *academic* drama, which had—or at least pretended to—a purely educational aim. No connection was admitted between it and the popular drama of the public theatre, which a few years later began to blossom so marvellously. To that, when it came a-visiting, the University would have nothing to say. In 1575 we find the Vice-Chancellor petitioning the Privy Council for powers to abate the nuisance of " ...the making of shows and playing of Interludes and setting forth of other vain games and pastimes... ". And the Privy Council sympathetically responds that " ...being informed very credibly of some attempts of light and decayed persons, who for filthy lucre are minded and do seek nowadays to devise and

[1] My reference is to Dr Boas' book on University Drama, the authoritative work on the whole subject.

set up in open places shows of unlawful, hurtful, pernicious and unhonest games near to that University of Cambridge... " they consider that " ...it cannot be but a great number of the youth and others of the same ['others of the same' must, I fear, mean the Dons] may be thereby enticed from their places of learning, to be beholders, learners and practisers of lewdness and unlawful acts... ".

It could not but be—and it was! For at least three of the undergraduates of that time, Christopher Marlowe, Robert Greene and Thomas Nashe, acquired a pronounced taste for the lewd practice of playwriting. And their pursuit of it when they went down had some consequence for the popular theatre, and, incidentally, made things no easier in this direction for the University. Since fifteen years later it is evident that the Privy Council has proved a broken reed (the Council, possibly, was disingenuous in these matters; it must, I think, have kept a Puritan clerk to write sympathetically to Vice-Chancellors and another to tell Alleyn and Burbage to go quietly ahead). By 1590, in any case, we find the University re-

6

duced to paying the Queen's Majesty's Players 20*s*. to "move on". It sounds terribly like blackmail. And that is not the worst. For in the same year we find travelling companies given 20*s*. and even 30*s*. to play before the Mayor and Corporation. We can only hope that no members of the University—graduate or undergraduate—slipped in disguised. However, as we know, the Puritans won in the end—and upon each front! They suppressed the academic theatre and the popular theatre too. And it has taken just about three hundred years for the drama to become a national art again.

I do not say that in the interval we have not had from time to time very first-rate drama of one sort or another. But it is worth noting that it has hardly ever been comprehensively first rate. Excellence in acting and excellence in playwriting have seldom coincided. It would be worth while also to ask why (B). Nor has the theatre, until once more to-day, ever, I think, shown the natural and unconscious strength, which can let us begin to call it a national art. At the Restoration its tragedy became artificial and its comedy a scandal to the average man

7

and woman. In the eighteenth century it was out of touch with life. In the nineteenth it was out of touch with literature too. That is the age of unactable closet dramas and unreadable plays. (The statement is, of course, too cursory. But it is not untrue.) But now we really seem to have something like a fresh upspringing of the art of the drama; very various in kind and quality, widespread certainly, and, I think, deep-rooted.

It has been of a most diverse growth. There was the development in the professional theatre, which you may date from the 1890's or a little earlier (C). This has produced the "modern English drama" of the textbooks. After the war comes the amateur dramatic movement; quite unlike the old pre-war "private theatricals"; not a parasite upon the professional theatre; and an essentially democratic movement. There has also been an astonishing rebirth of the religious drama. Finally—and this to me is the most gratifying thing of all—we have what one may call the new Humanism in education turning, as did the old Humanism, to the art of drama. But not this time as master to servant;

8

rather as if seeking alliance upon terms of mutual respect. Everywhere to-day in schools we have some use of the dramatic method (as it is called) in teaching, and the acting of plays encouraged. In the Universities we no longer have to add the respectable "literature" to make the dangerous "dramatic" tolerable. Drama may show itself for what it is. And here, as we see, is the great University of Cambridge reconciled not only to drama as drama but to its old enemy the popular theatre also.

That is, fundamentally, a far healthier state of things. Drama is drama, even as music is music; no matter the kind or the quality. Beethoven's great Mass is music; but so is the tune vamped on a penny whistle at the street corner. *King Lear* and the *Agamemnon* are drama; but so is the silliest farce or a charade in the nursery. By that, as a principle, one must abide. For it is in their wide range that the power of the two arts lies; in the fact that, either as musician and actor on the one hand or listener and spectator on the other, we may pass from the penny whistle and the charade to the Mass and *King Lear*, if we have the talent or the taste to do so, nothing hindering us. And since beside this they are *social* arts, they are the two that it best becomes a democracy to cultivate. They have, of course, their divisions and branches, their nobler and meaner aspects. But these in themselves are, so to speak, natural divisions; therefore it is profitable to distinguish them. What is not profitable is to set up arbitrary and snobbish divisions; to have the "classic" musician despising the mere tune-maker—or *vice versa*; or, as was proved three centuries ago, an academic drama snubbing the popular. Nevertheless, from the academic point of view, if relations are to be intimate, and when it comes to admitting drama as drama into the curriculum of a school or a university, the most liberal of Humanists will have some practical questions to ask.

How precisely is the drama to be turned to educational use? Is it to be a thing of general or only of specialised study? And—as important a question, perhaps—how is its misuse to be prevented?

For (let us be frank about it) the drama, or rather the theatre, can be a very enthralling pursuit for young people; an exciting and, with other duller but possibly more important studies in view, a dangerously distracting pursuit. And if it is to be a recognised pursuit—well, though the mountain-tops in view are magnificent the earning a living among them is hard; while the lowlands, where anyone it seems may cultivate and build, are only too temptingly fertile. For there is a lot of marshy land that may be lighted on; and there are will-o'-the-wisps about. In plain terms, no school or university will want to see its recognition of the drama made the means of sending hundreds of young men and young women rushing recklessly into the uncertain world of the theatre; where, while youth and good looks and vitality are at a premium, middle-age and mere experience are too often disastrously at a discount; where success at twenty-five may well mean failure at fifty—and vain regrets (D). Therefore, if this new alliance between education and the drama is to be a lasting one, education will need to be sure that from her point of view the terms of the treaty are suitable. The question has come to need consideration; and I will try to suggest a few items of an imaginary agenda for its discussion.

Of the present use of drama in schools I do not know enough even to ask intelligent questions. But here in Cambridge we do not have to go far for information about that. What the Perse School has done in this kind must be famous the educational world over. And it is pretty generally granted, I think, that "the dramatic method", which takes advantage of and cultivates the dramatic instinct in a child, may be a help to teaching in general and is without doubt the best approach to the study of drama itself. And the actual acting of plays will certainly help children to move well and speak well, will give them that old-fashioned and underrated thing called "deportment"; and that newer-fashioned, and perhaps for the moment overrated, thing called "self-expression". This may be—it is, I am sure—excellent and sufficient for children. But it does not follow that a mere elaboration of the practice will suffice or even suit the adolescent and the adult.

There appeared in *The Times* a few weeks ago an interesting communication from Professor

Allardyce Nicoll upon American universities
and their encouragement of the drama. He has
lately become head of the famous School of the
Theatre at Yale, founded thirty years ago or
more—but at Harvard—by Professor George
Pierce Baker, who has now retired. This school,
incidentally, is still an exceptional institution;
though many others have drawn inspiration
from it. Its work is mainly post-graduate. It
is a laboratory where dramatic art, with its
contributory arts, can be studied as a whole and
in parts, can be both studied and experimentally
practised. It is a very remarkable institution.
And I am convinced that as far as the credit
for a nation-wide movement can be given to
one institution and one man, America owes her
extraordinary advance in the art of the theatre
during this past quarter of a century to that
school and to George Pierce Baker. But Professor Allardyce Nicoll speaks mainly of the way
in which undergraduates in American universities generally are encouraged to act and given
academic credit for doing so. "The stage performances", he says, "are welcomed because
they provide opportunities for acquiring ease,

13

grace of diction, and practical understanding of dramatic masterpieces." He says that in fact they are looked upon "much in the same way as the early humanists considered the performance of Latin plays by their pupils".

Now this is very well. I am not—needless to say—against the acting of plays in a university. I rejoice in it; but chiefly as a symbol of the drama's emancipation there, far less because of its utility. I have been a guest at many American universities; and one can have little but admiration for their response to the impatient hunger of their students for every sort of intellectual experience—a hunger which in itself contrasts very favourably with what could (once upon a time) be more commonly remarked here; a certain youthful reluctance to fall upon the outspread feast! (E) I agree, too, that this acting is a good way of acquiring ease and grace; though we should rather be talking of "maintaining the ease and grace already acquired". For, if our schools do their due share, young men and women ought no more to come to a university unable to walk, talk and express themselves properly than unable to spell or add

14

two and two together. But while acting in them may give an actor much of the "practical understanding of dramatic masterpieces" which, as an actor, he needs, this is not the sort of knowledge, I should say, which the adult student of drama most needs to acquire, nor even the best approach to it. Here, in fact, is a distinction which it is important to make clear: between the way of the apprentice which is the best way for those who mean to give their lives to the *practice* of an art; and the critical approach of the student whose object is to *appreciate* it.

It is true that many people—though by no means all—come most easily even to appreciative terms with an art by practising it a little. A little amateur acting, producing, even playwriting, will certainly teach us the alphabet of the affair, habituate us to the language of drama (though for this, as we saw, our school days should provide). But it will not necessarily take us very far in appreciating the great works written in that language. It may even—if we are not careful—hinder us from going further. We do not want with the drama to slip into the fallacy which for a few generations associated a knowledge of music with the playing of a few tunes on the piano. There is danger in confusing study with accomplishment. It is the danger of passing from "Now I can do this" to "Then there is no more to do"; the danger of contracting one's vision of an art to the measure of one's own capacities. A particular danger this, in the case of dramatic art, of which the rudiments are so simple that a child can grasp them. Almost anybody can write a play—of a sort! And literally anybody can act—in a way!

Anybody can act. But the highly developed *art* of acting is a very difficult art indeed. It does not consist simply in pretending to be somebody you are not. Nor, obviously, can it be *self*-expression, though that is a part of the training for it. The definition is inadequate; but we could call it the expressing of the dramatist's idea in terms of the actor's personality, or the playing of a tune upon the complex and uncertain instrument which is one's physical, emotional and intellectual self. And that is only the beginning of the business. There is the problem of giving to this composite

16

and alien creature, when you have embodied it, adequate expression within the narrow limits of time and opportunity which are all that the longest play and part can afford. There is the still harder problem of reconciling this expression with the equal need for expression of the other characters in the play. For a good actor is one who not only gives himself utterly to his own part but is responsive enough to his fellows to help them play theirs. No, it is not an easy art. And, beyond a few illuminating hints dropped by actors themselves, not much—as far as I know—that is helpful has been written about it. Diderot's neat paradox only serves to show that the problem begins where his understanding of it leaves off. I rather wonder that our latest oracles, the scientific psychologists, have not dealt with the matter. (Perhaps I speak ignorantly, and they have.) For certainly its secrets lie somewhere in that realm of the subconscious over which they have hoisted their flag. I am not sure, however, that I want the actor and his art psycho-analysed. A performance of *Hamlet* fresh from a Freudian Laboratory—I fancy one would hate it! No;

possibly we had better leave to the occult and inconsequent methods of the artist this exercise in applied psychology which is the **art** of acting (**F**).

Even if it were the right approach for him, I do not fancy that the average student, with another chief aim in life, would go far along this path. And it will be a pity if his use of the rudiments of acting as a sort of aesthetic gymnastic should inhibit his appreciation of true acting, which—though it is not the whole art of drama —is still an important part of it, by which, indeed, we are most naturally led to appreciate the art as a whole. A little indulgence in acting may help us to like drama better; but for its study we need a more impersonal approach.

There is the natural one, of seeing a supremely good play superbly acted. We can recommend that to any student—when the combination is available! Unfortunately it is not, so very often. Besides, though this would show him (if he might take our word for it) what good drama was, it would not tell him *why* it was good. Even the most expert cannot always see the play itself quite clearly through the veil of a

18

performance of it, dispelling from his mind the illusion the acting induces—if that is good, or replacing it in imagination with good acting—if it is bad. We have to give our student an instructive view of the play itself. We do not mean to fall back again upon the mere printed page. What we want, I suggest, is some plan which will give a play as much life as will let us study it in being, yet not so much as will set it free of our critical control. We want to be able to keep it for a while in a state of incubation. I daresay the very obvious plan that follows is already pretty generally employed. My arguments may then serve to justify it.

What may suit us, then—let me try now to put it in a phrase—is a method of studying a play involving all the preparations for a performance which we know from the beginning we shall never have to give. We shall choose one, of course, that has matter in it for study; there are many, excellent in themselves and in their kind, that obviously have not. But let us take it that we are to study *Hamlet*. We must first have done with talk about text; about the First Quarto; the comparative value of the Second

Quarto and the Folio. You do not begin to prepare a play for performance till its text is pretty definitely settled. You do not, that is to say, unless you are guilty of the dangerous heresy that there is a kind of absolute art of the theatre, the task of which is not simply to interpret the author's play, but to re-create it in its own terms.

May I digress for a moment upon a painful subject? I do not know how many people consciously and contumaciously hold that damnable belief to-day. The germ of it can be traced to the days before the war. But it was then of a mild and merely philosophic nature, and could even be profitably discussed—in private! For, like most soul-destroying doctrines, it has a grain of truth in it; enough to make it attractive and to lead the unwary astray. And in the moral and intellectual anarchy which followed the war it inevitably found fertile soil. It spread like a plague. Many promising young producers were led by it to destruction. The more opinionated of them became Presentationalists and Conditionalists and Subjective Illusionists and other such furiously-sounding and (possibly) *some*thing-signifying things. Like most revolutionary movements it has had its destructive usefulness. The old heavily upholstered staging has, one hopes, finally vanished. And—though I think this chiefly reflected the heavily upholstered life of the time, and with that was passing—I will not grudge our heretics a share in the credit of the destruction. The less, since the fantastic symbolism with which they wished to replace it is vanishing in its turn. For, however momentarily amusing they may be to look at, are these contrivances of coloured lights and ladders and little platforms, splashes of paint and geometrical nightmares—are they dramatically creative? What have they created that we can put a name to at the end of a performance?

Creative acting I find a little more comprehensible than creative scenery. One recalls the Commedia dell' Arte. Yet that had given themes on which to improvise. One thinks of the clown in the circus. He was acclaimed by our bright young heretics a few years ago as the greatest of dramatic artists. I fear they have forgotten him lately. What is all this, however, but a return to the primitive art from which the drama sprang? And as in dramatic history, so with this heresy, the dramatist creeps into partnership. Our heretics will admit him—on their own terms. He may contribute his share, provide some material for scene-designer and actor to re-create. Well, if the bargain is an honest one, if the dramatist goes in (so to speak) with his eyes open, why should we complain? I do not—of this! I only remark that the partnership has not upon these terms produced any very vital drama so far; drama, that is to say, of any *re*-productive promise. I hold myself that it cannot hope to; since to exalt the theatre, as this heresy does, at the expense of the drama is a retrograde step. But what I do complain of is the misuse of plays which were never meant to be submitted to this theatrically creative treatment, which ask merely to be honestly and modestly interpreted. There is nothing, as far as I can see, to justify the translating of the *Agamemnon* into modern slang, his entry riding on a tank flanked by machine guns; or a symbolic staging of *Hedda Gabler*; or the playing of Othello as a puppet

22

jerked about by Iago; or such a performance of *Hamlet* as is reported from Russia, with Hamlet himself as a comic character and the play twisted into a mockery of the ridiculous morality of the bourgeoisie. Such aberrations are not even honestly funny. We have escaped the worst of them in England, and I think the danger is now over. But at any sign of an outbreak stern measures should be taken. A day in the pillory for the producer and the loss of his ears might be sufficient punishment. But I should be for severer treatment if necessary.

To return, however, to our own imaginary and very humble task of the mere study of this particular play.

We must know the sort of stage upon which we are *not* going to perform it. For we certainly cannot visualise it in action otherwise. The usages of the Elizabethan stage in general and their dramatic purpose—these, I take it, are now within the knowledge of every student. But since they were never very rigid there is always room to discuss how they apply to certain junctures in any particular play. And the discussion may be quite enlightening. In

Hamlet, for instance, the relations of the King and Queen may be sensibly affected by the construction we put upon the confused stage directions at the end of the closet scene. And only the other day I argued for an hour with Professor Dover Wilson as to precisely where and how the Ghost scenes were acted. I did not convince him; nor he me! Incidentally, I believe I might have had a better chance with him had there been a large-scale model of the Globe Theatre to hand. And that (let us note), even though it has to be upon some minor points an imaginary and disputed reconstruction, should always be available for such study as we are considering. Every school and college where Elizabethan drama is seriously studied should have a half-inch or, better, an inch model of an Elizabethan theatre.

The question of costume? This, in so far as it relates to Shakespeare's own vision of the characters, we must go into. But, as we are not to make costumes or wear them, we need not go very far.

We come soon enough, in fact, to the essential step of bringing the characters to life, imagining them in action. By the purely physical action we need not be much troubled. Let the purpose and general trend be clear, it does not matter to the student (it should matter very little to the actor) whether such and such a character is supposed to be standing here or there, or gesticulating with his right arm or his left. In any play worth calling a play the physical action will always be the least important part. It lives by virtue of its intellectual and emotional conflict. And only the imagined embodiment of the characters is needed to set this going. Here our method of concerted study begins to justify itself. For it is just at this point that the imaginative powers of the solitary reader, and the interpretative powers of the lecturer, are apt to fail. Neither may appreciate to the full the dramatic value which lies in the conflict or even the mere opposition of character. The singly working mind will rather take a middle way, the way of the narrator of a story— and turn our play into one of those Tales from Shakespeare which Lamb made so charming. It is hard even for the most expert to imagine to the full the effect of this embodied conflict of character. Even the dramatist who has devised it may find unexpected turns in it when it comes into being. But since this, revealing character as only conflict can (in art as in life), is the very essence of drama, it must somehow be realised. And it should be made the mainspring of our study.

That implies a distributing of parts among the students. Yet I still would not cast the play as if for a performance; each part definitely allotted to its actor. I would, to begin with, follow the economical Elizabethan example of doubling (and trebling and quadrupling) the smaller parts. Then, I think, I would divide my class into two teams: one to embody the play while the other listened and criticised; each taking its turn at either task. There are several advantages in this. For one: the more vital a character in a play the greater the variety of the embodiment that can be given it. Its life will be deeply rooted; and we shall only appreciate how deeply by varying the outward expression. We shall better distinguish the essential by recognising the inessentials. There are fifty different ways of playing Hamlet; each, that is to say, may show some salient difference. But if Hamlet is at the heart of them they will none of them be wrong.

Then (even though we are to have no performance) you cannot quite bring a play to life without allowing for an audience. Actors play *to* each other, but they are playing *for* an audience. When they rehearse, the producer impersonates the audience; an ideally critical audience (G). Without a sounding-board of this sort, our students will find their projecting of the characters—though they may not guess why—falling rather flat. Again, the play itself must be criticised. And here is a capital difference between this sort of study and the preparation of a play for performance. Study includes the obligation to criticise, performance the obligation not to. A company rehearsing must very soon drop its critical attitude towards a play. For if the actors cannot, when it comes to the point, quite uncritically identify themselves with their parts their performance will be a very inhuman affair. Here also will be a test of the play's repayment of this intensive study. If it is one of those whose performance involves a conspiracy by the actors to persuade us that it is a better play than it is, a play that asks its actors not only to embody the characters, but to endow them with essential individuality too, we shall be wasting our time. One may roughly divide plays into the two categories, of those that are so far dependent upon their actors and those that are not. It is not always easy to distinguish between the two off-hand. This "lively study" will bring both sorts to life. But criticism will kill the first, and it will not kill the second sort (H).

It will not kill *Hamlet*. I have heard talk of *Hamlet* being an artistic failure. But I suspect that in this case the critic was able to kill the play to his own satisfaction because he had not brought it to life first. He must indeed have taken some solitary pains actually to prevent it coming to life, since it is one of the very liveliest of plays. Yet there is much be-praised drama which will, we shall find, utterly succumb under this treatment. It should perhaps, therefore, be submitted to it.

And what should be the end of this process of study? There can in one sense be no end (if the play survives its criticism). We must break off when we have had enough. And we should always be left well aware that this study of a play, however lively and thorough, is in its nature an incomplete thing. Completion comes with performance. And that is a theatre's business.

Must we provide a theatre, then, in which the process may be completed, where the play will be performed, if not by these students—whom we have supposed to be taking "drama" as one among a dozen other subjects—by others for whom it is a special subject, or by professionals?

Let me again make it clear that I am all for student performances; as many as the authorities (with other interests to consider) will allow time for and the available audiences endure; also that I recognise "the fresh and unspoiled beauty" of some of these compared with "the stale trickiness" which the professional actor would bring to them—or, to be exact, I *have* occasionally recognised it. But I fear that we are all too easily led into canting a little about that sort of thing. What I want to insist on is that these performances are no substitute for critical study. And it is to critical study that we must chiefly look for the creation of an audience which will appreciate—and demand—good drama. And that is the true end at which to aim.

I should be very glad to see established in some one English university—possibly in two, but not more—such a laboratory of post-graduate study for men and women out to become actors, producers, decorators or playwrights, as that founded by Professor Baker at Yale. And there fairly frequent performances would quite rightly be given.

I should like to see—and heaven knows why we should not see—a professional theatre in every university town, linked to the university by delegates on its board of directors, who would have the usual directors' say in its conduct and its programmes. There is one already at Liverpool, if not ostensibly linked with the university, grateful, I am sure, for its goodwill. And, fortunately, Mr William Armstrong, its very able director, is later to talk to you about it. Nothing could be simpler than to set up such a theatre in every university town in England. If it were intelligently directed it would need but a comparatively modest grant-in-aid to balance its finances. The accounts of the quite promising experiments already made should be evidence of that. If they have not been financially profitable, no one has lost a fortune by them. And why should not this sort of a theatre, as well as a museum or a picture gallery, be allowed to reckon its profits in other terms than finance? (I)

But I do not want to bring our plan to the logical conclusion that the students must see— even if they are not to partake in—a performance of each play they study. One should beware of too much logic in such matters. Nor am I now so concerned with the establishing of particular theatres as with the relation of the study of the drama to the theatre in general; since the new aspect of this—as this meeting shows—is a capital feature of the whole present situation. Nor, again, do I want to see too close and logical a link forged between the two *aspects* of drama; of its use in education, and as entertainment in a theatre. For there is—so I have contended—some natural incompatibility here. Not with regard to the drama itself;

that was the error of the sixteenth-century Humanists, who envisaged two Dramas instead of one. Ah, had they but preferred Shakespeare to Seneca, the history of England itself might have been a little different! But as to the means of turning it to account. Here, if I am right, the ways of the artist and the student, though now and then they meet, run in the main apart.

You may remember that Monsieur Bergeret, when he was hanging the pictures in his new apartment, sought for the reason of the pleasure it gave him to drive nails into walls. And, says Anatole France, he found the reason, but he lost the pleasure; for perhaps we enjoy things most when we enjoy them without knowing the reason why. Which, if not a profound truth, is a warning to the serious minded! And its application here is that we do not want, by conferring academic importance on the drama, to vitiate it in our students' eyes—or our own—as an entertainment. For drama in the theatre should be an entertainment. And even the drama that is much more should be consistently entertaining too; as it can legitimately be made. Its other qualities apart, there is, of course, as

32

much sheer entertainment in *Hamlet* as in any farce. And if I thought that by telling a man to study this play or another I was lessening his power to enjoy it in the theatre I should be disposed to leave him in a happier ignorance. But this—despite Monsieur Bergeret—is not the alternative forced upon us, if ——! If the theatre will now do its part, and make of its entertainment the true completion and the crown of our study.

The friendly gesture made after three centuries by this University to the theatre is also, I think—and legitimately so—a gesture of demand. It says in effect to the theatre: "Our functions in the matter are different, but they are complementary. And though our study may be of some use to *us*, it will not be of great use to the *art* of the drama—it may even do this some harm, by making the best of it seem too academic a thing—unless you can match the study by your entertainment; unless, indeed, you can outmatch it, leave it in the shade, so transcend it that you will make it (what in fact it is meant only to be) a preparation for the uncalculating enjoyment of the glamour and the glory of the art itself. But that, surely, the theatre, with all its resources, with men and women devoting their lives to it, *can* do". And this friendly gesture is, in fact, a veritable challenge which, even for its own sake, the theatre must take up.

We cannot pretend it is being very fully answered now. You will be talked to during this coming fortnight about a score of masterpieces, and another score or so of good plays of the past or the present. But if in London this autumn you go the round of the ordinary theatres expecting performances of them which will justify the lecturers' enthusiasm, or, indeed, of the greater part of them any performances at all, it will prove a disappointing round.

Yet the theatre is, I believe, at least conscious of this new challenge; and, in the face of extraordinary difficulties, is struggling to answer it. In so far as it fails to, it will be helpful to distinguish just what the failure is and where the blame for it lies. Not, to begin with, in any primary lack of competence and goodwill among the better part of the actors; who indeed are not only always ready to do the best work they can find, but will wear out their strength by flinging themselves enthusiastically into one forlorn hope after another. Miraculously, their enthusiasm survives. I trust that the last of that foolish legend is dissipated, which painted the average actor as a vain, lazy and luxurious child. He will not have, perhaps, the brains of a first-rate philosopher or scientist, a lawyer or financier—but then he has not chosen those paths in life! He is as fond of luxury as the rest of us, and in these days as little able to afford it. When he is hard at work there is no more nervously exhausting work that I know of. If he did not keep that something of the child in him which all artists have he could not be an actor at all. Writers, painters, musicians may keep this childlikeness hidden from their public, however. He cannot. As to vanity, there is obviously no calling so likely to breed it. Yet for his work's sake he will listen calmly to comments besides which the sergeant-major's talk to the latest recruit is mere flattery. I have, indeed, found his vanity compare very favourably to that of the man of letters; yes, even to the scientist's. Theirs, when they are afflicted by it, is intellectual and pernicious, while the actor's, after all, evaporates in attitudes and superficial emotion. No, for what may be lacking in the theatre to-day the actor is not primarily to blame. Nor are the producers of plays. Nor even—altogether—the managers of theatres, who must pay rents and make profits as other shopkeepers must. For what they have to manage are, indeed, not really theatres, but shops—for the display of the latest dramatic novelties. Here, I think, is the root of the trouble. The ordinary London theatre to-day exists by catering to the public appetite for sensation and novelty. The question a manager will ask when he finds a play is not so much whether it is in itself good or bad as whether it is in the fashion of the moment, or, if he has unusual *flair*, whether it may not set a fashion for the coming moment.

Now—the question of profit and loss apart—there is nothing unnatural in this attitude on the part of theatre managers. For the art of the theatre is, in itself, an ephemeral thing. No other art—except, for some of us, music—has such power over the moment. And none can present to us such an intensification of life. But it pays the very price that life pays. The moment passes, and nothing remains but our unaided memory of it. It may be just this, indeed, which gives the theatre a peculiar place in our affections—when it has any at all. The occasions of no account are easily forgotten and what remains is intimately our own. But the art of the dramatist can acquire the enduring value of literature. Certainly, its methods change with the times, but no more quickly. What is poor will perish; but the best can survive—as even the very best in the theatre cannot—to link the past with the present, to establish tradition, and a standard by which it and the theatre that interprets it may be appreciated. It is the drama which, we may almost say, gives to the theatre its immortal soul. And we ought not to have to think of the two apart. The present trouble is that our "standard" theatre (so to call it; and there is no other that is generally efficient) does not represent the drama, or attempt to. Compare your student's knowledge of the one with—as I say—the season's programme of the other. Such variety as you find (and in appearance there is so much that my remark may surprise you) is superficial, a mask to the fundamental sameness of any fashionable thing (J). The theatre's ephemeral interests prevail even to the prejudice of the drama it does purvey to us, even to its own; since—with fashion for sole guide—neither can profit by the past nor provide for the future. For all the use it is to the theatre of to-day, the drama of the last fifty years might never have been written. And the waste goes on. As good plays are being written, it may be; but good and bad alike, when they have served their turn, are thrown aside and forgotten. We win victories, but we never consolidate our gains. What demoralises the theatre to-day is the fact that work for it, however fine, however devoted, is but a ploughing of the sands. No art can be cultivated, nor any intelligent public kept faithful to it, upon such terms.

The remedy is simple. The majority of the theatres in a great city only need be concerned with the drama of the moment. This can be excellent in its kind; and, indeed, the very greatest plays were once the drama of the moment, since the dramatist who pretends to write for posterity generally misses that mark also. All that is needed is for two or three theatres—or as many more as may find a public—to be organised in the *permanent interests* of the drama. It does not matter what we call the theatres; National, Municipal or Repertory. Nor is there any one way to organise them (though there are several ways *not* to). We only need to keep their purpose in mind, and to realise that the more permanent interests of the drama cannot be identical—even though the two things may occasionally coincide—with its exploiting for the maximum financial profit of the moment.

You may think that I am ungratefully forgetting the enthusiasm and money which have recently gone to the endowing of "Shakespeare" theatres. I am not. It is a good beginning. But it would, I must point out, be a very bad ending.

Shakespeare is the greatest figure in our drama—possibly in all drama! But we do the English drama in general, and Shakespeare himself in particular, a mere disservice by separating him from the rest of it, treating him as a god and building temples to him in which he only is to be worshipped. That sort of worship soon degenerates into superstition; and in these very theatres we may note the familiar signs of this degeneracy already appearing. What else is the extravagantly decorative ritual, which the high priests—the producers—have now begun to elaborate there? Do they fear their disciples may soon be bored by the simple worship of the god himself? They have cause to fear it. There are honest worshippers, I know. But there are the snobs and the hypocrites also. My sympathies are with them; it asks courage to refuse to conform. They have their punishment, however; for Shakespeare ritualised, is, as soon as the novelty wears off, far more boring than the simple thing itself can ever be. The truth is that we do not want an exclusively Shakespearean theatre—no, not even at Stratford!—where the performance of his plays becomes a ritual, plain or extravagant, to be carried out by "Shakespearean" actors, who will, in this unnatural confinement, first earn the reputation of being able to act nothing else, and then lose even that. We want a theatre (and more than one) in which Shakespeare merely has the place that is his in the whole rich landscape of English drama—of pre-eminence and abiding inspiration. Then it will mean something to everyone concerned, dramatists, producers, actors, to find *their* places even in the most modest corner of it. And his supreme art will be a reinforcement to the rest, no longer be held up as a sort of reproach to it. We begin to do Shakespeare himself, I say, a disservice in so isolating him. For this new natural feeling for the drama in England is a feeling for it as a whole, and for drama itself, not for any reputations already made in it, even the greatest. And in this lies its true strength, and the best hope for the future.

I suggest, indeed, to the patient promoters of the Shakespeare National Theatre that they are now rather handicapped than helped by a too close association of his name with their project. It is even possible that there is a little too much talk in general about Shakespeare at the moment. And as I am one of the culprits it is perhaps not unbecoming for me to say so.

I undertake to stop soon. There is a saturation point in everything. We are passing into a phase of having less to say about him than about our own and each other's ideas about him; it is another aspect of the producer's extravagant ritual. If we go on much longer we may—critics and producers both—be brought back to common sense by a sharp reactionary shock.

But taking it by and large, the situation of the drama in England to-day is a very hopeful one. At the base of the pyramid, so to speak, we have the use of drama in the schools; and this widespread popular taste—which really seems to be more than a passing craze—for amateur acting. There is the Church's reconciliation, at which I have not even been able to glance; but Mr Laurence Housman is to speak about it, with far more knowledge than I have. A most important thing socially! For the Puritan prejudice, which once closed the theatres altogether, is by no means dead. It showed only the other day when (other excellent reasons being given—for Puritanism is no longer a term of pride) it prevented them, though it could not prevent the cinemas, from being opened on

Sunday (K). But we have lived to see a play written by the Poet Laureate performed in Canterbury Cathedral itself; and—more significant still!—the Puritans of Milton's mind and Falkland's and Marvell's, the finer mind of Puritan Humanism, acquiesced and approved. Then there is the reconciliation with the Universities and all they stand for, which we have been discussing. This carries the pyramid up a long way.

We have, then, a public appreciation of the art by practice and study unexampled in our history and (America apart) in any other country. It remains for the professional theatre —which itself shows an unprecedented liveliness and enterprise at least—to cap the pyramid by entertaining us with the quality and extent of drama which we have learned to appreciate. And though the organisation here needed involves the breaking down of a few remaining prejudices (mainly economic), I do not—may I say, even after thirty years of pleading for it?—I do not despair.

In fact, while, the world over, we hear voices loudly despairing of democracy and calling out for tyrants to do for us what we thus seem to be too witless to do for ourselves, I notice that England, in her slow, hesitating, compromising and quite exasperating way, distrustful of theories, worried by the names of things, as determined as ever to do nothing thoroughly, is yet working out, one by one, to each its solution, the problems which our latest social revolution has left us to solve. The new age is crowded and complex, and much has to be organised, which we could more happily let alone before. The theatre, in any case, has to be organised: it is the one art which cannot escape it. I do not doubt that its turn will come (L). Not for an ideal organisation (the two words hardly belong together) but for one that will "do the job".

Do I maintain that this of itself will bring us a new creative golden age of drama? Not for a moment! Such events have deeper and more mysterious springs. But it will, at least, let us enjoy the riches that we have. And it may be that these immaterial riches are what we are coming the more to value, since the solider sort has of late shown such a strange tendency to crumble and disappear. It may also be that this is the less heroic task marked out for the next few generations: to conserve those things of spiritual quality, which our civilisation has produced, as a witness for it to posterity when—and who knows how soon—the rest of it shall have passed away.

NOTES

Page 2 (A) *In Cambridge...semi-private performances...and...the existence of an amateur club, were tolerated....*

The early history of the Cambridge A.D.C. itself
may be studied in F. C. Burnand's rollicking
book on the subject. Nor should the historian
of the Nineteenth Century professional theatre
neglect to note the influence of this Cambridge
tributary to the main stream. For Burnand the
drama was a "lark", and his standard of its
excellence, to end as to begin with, *Box and Cox*
and the like. He edited *Punch*, was still editing
it when the new movement in the theatre—the
"Ibsen Movement" as it was called—began; so
he would both form and reflect conventional
English opinion upon that. And at least one
other Cantabrigian eddy can be distinguished
in the stream. Among the members of the
A.D.C. in the late eighteen seventies are the
Hon. C. R. Spencer and Mr Charles H. E.
Brookfield. In November 1878 Mr Spencer
acted Mrs Chesterton in J. Maddison Morton's
John Dobbs; Mr Brookfield, James Dalton in
Tom Taylor's *The Ticket-of-leave Man.*

In 1909 Mr Spencer is Earl Spencer, Lord Chamberlain and Licenser of plays, and he appoints Mr Charles Brookfield as his Reader. Where should he find a man more of his own mind? But the appointment, as naturally, scandalises the adherents of the new movement, who are already loud in their protest at the Lord Chamberlain's refusal to license one "pioneer" play after another. For Mr Brookfield is a famous adapter of "risky" French farces and has just produced a none too "refined" version of Labiche's *Célimène le bien-aimé*. A pretty sort of moral watch-dog! Whereupon—though this was but one of the causes—we have the Parliamentary Select Committee on the Censorship, and a full-dress battle between the "new" drama and the old conventions and restrictions, in which the "new" drama vindicates its cause—and is beaten. Values have changed since then; see how the descriptive epithets must be set in inverted commas! The disputed plays are all licensed, and others are licensed now by which the "new" dramatists grown old are somewhat shocked. And Wycherley's *The Country Wife* (which Garrick had to bowdlerise) runs unexpurgated for a hundred nights and more at a London theatre! The humour of this is, of course, that Wycherley

48

does not need a licence. And one of the posers commonly put twenty-five years ago to the defenders of the Censor as moral watch-dog was: And what if any manager tried to produce *The Country Wife*?; the answer being: The thing is unthinkable. But the question of the Censorship is still to be settled—and will have to be at some time or other. Therefore it may still be worth remarking that the old protest was not against the licensing of *Célimène le bien-aimé* (an amusing farce, for which anyone's moral digestion should be strong enough, though in its English dress it became rather depressingly vulgar) but against the concurrent refusal of Ibsen's *Ghosts*, Maeterlinck's *Monna Vanna*, Shelley's *The Cenci* and a dozen other plays "of good intent".

Brookfield, it may be added for those who did not know him, was a man of much brilliance as an actor and—or, at least, he might have been—as a dramatic writer too. But his career came to little, largely because there was no theatre to stretch his talents to their utmost. And for such a theatre he thought there was no use! The Cambridge of to-day might have brought him to think otherwise. Incidentally, his sharp tongue apart, he was a very kindly man. He proved so in the early nineties to a professionally

friendless youth who was then battling his way
into the theatre, who fifteen years later much
disliked to find himself ranged against the man,
and seemingly forgetful of that early kindness.
Not that this would surprise or trouble Brookfield; or, if it did, one stinging sentence would
relieve his feelings.

Page 7 (B) *Excellence in acting and excellence
in playwriting have not coincided. It would
be worth while also to ask why.*

The lecturer was indeed here tempted to go off
at a tangent and spend the rest of his time in
asking why. He does not quite know the answer.
But he does know that this is the master-problem
of the theatre: how to retain great acting in the
service of great plays. In their *service*; for, however great the actor, if the play is worthy of
great acting we should be left thinking more of
it than we think of him.

Page 8 (C) *There was the development in the
professional theatre, which you may date
from the 1890's or a little earlier.*

It is often dated from T. W. Robertson and the
late sixties. I would say nothing to diminish
Robertson's peculiar credit. But after *Caste* he

did not improve upon himself; and after his death in 1871 the drama seems for a while to be rather at sixes and sevens; though such a sympathetic and purposeful critic as William Archer can (in his *English Dramatists of To-day*, 1882) discern hopeful tendencies. What *is* observable, however, is the recruiting and training, under the Bancrofts, the Kendals, Hare and Wyndham, of a new generation of actors who will be more competent to deal with a modern English drama when this is provided them. And in the nineties, Pinero, Henry Arthur Jones, Carton, Grundy and the rest begin to push forward and provide it.

Page 11 (D) ...*the uncertain world of the theatre ...where success at twenty-five may well mean failure at fifty....*

But what a change in forty years! Once a young man drifted into the theatre because he was of no use elsewhere, or took to it enthusiastically despite parental head-shakings, with the prospect that when he was "resting"—and he would often be "resting"; the euphemism, this, for being out of a job—his friends and relations would have to support him. Now, let him be the rather more than personable son of a

Bishop or an Under-Secretary of State and he may easily, after a success or so, better his father's wretched £3000 a year. Truly it is rather the cinema than the theatre which will be ready to buy his photogenic good looks at that price; and, as I say, he may soon enough discover that there is another aspect to the business. But, equally, he may not! The old method of recruiting left much to be desired; but this sort of extravagance it is which is largely responsible for the present financial demoralisation of the theatre as a whole.

Page 14 (E) *I have been a guest at many American universities; and one can have little but admiration for their response to the impatient hunger of their students. . . .*

They are conscious in America both of the more and less admirable aspects of this anxiety to learn and the responsive readiness to teach anything and everything. I once heard the Dean of Williams College (one of the older and more conservative institutions of New England) tell a Commencement audience that a young man had recently written from the Middle West demanding a course of study which would carry him "by easy stages through Landscape

52

Gardening, Concrete Construction and Law ".
We all laughed uproariously. But I felt later
that while I, for my part, certainly preferred
Williams with its strict old-fashioned insistence
upon the Humanities, yet that there was something admirable, if pathetic, in this young man's
notion that, somewhere in the cultured East,
such an Eldorado of assorted learning must
surely exist. Note, besides, that very gallant
projects for a career are implied in the outrageous demand—outrageous, but there may
well be American universities ready to satisfy it !
He is to earn his bread by Landscape Gardening
and Concrete Construction while he slowly
drives his way through the more dignified but
doubtless more resistant study of Law.

Page 18 (F) *No; possibly we had better leave to
the occult and inconsequent methods of the
artist this exercise in applied psychology
which is the art of acting.*

Dare I suggest that, upon this side of the
pathological, psychology is more the artist's
business than the scientist's ? Freud—or rather
Freudianism—has so far been a damnable influence upon drama, and, I rather suspect, upon
imaginative literature in general. But how resist

53

such tempting opportunities as here offered? A new and most sensational field of psychological operations, neatly mapped out by Science and popularised by its camp-followers! The subconscious self! But the fact is that all the greater writers have been dealing with the subconscious since imaginative literature began. They have not so labelled it, nor given it, indeed, any imagination-saving label. For them it has been an integral part of the individual mystery; dark and difficult to penetrate, and interwoven with the spiritual mystery, something, therefore, to be sensitively, even reverently approached.

But thanks to the New Psychology we need now put ourselves to no such trouble. Here are "cases" for us, row upon row of them, the "reactions" of the patients all tabulated, the cure prescribed. Our would-be Shakespeare of to-day, with a Hamlet for his subject, has only to note that the wretched fellow was suffering from an Oedipus-complex and the mystery is solved. Why does no one take Shakespeare's *Hamlet* (as Shakespeare possibly took Kyd's) and rewrite it on these lines? Let Claudius, whose mind and conscience even as we have them are most supple, allow Hamlet to return to Wittenberg (it is never made clear why he did not), where some psycho-analyst must surely await him. He can return in the next act freed from the doubts and hesitations which so intolerably prolong the present play. Whether he will not also have been freed from belief in the Ghost and the need to revenge his father, that is for our would-be Shakespeare to decide. But the theme will at least have been lifted to a more enlightened plane; and we shall be spared those useless reflections upon duty and honour, death and immortality, matters upon which even the New Psychology has nothing very new to say.

Freudianism can be a great help to the critic too. I have recently been told that Othello was a "Narcissist", because, while Desdemona loved him for the dangers he had passed, he loved her because she pitied them. There is likewise skulking about some queerly obscene explanation of the relations between Lear and Cordelia. Would "dirty nonsense" be too strong a term for such talk? I do not use the "dirty" abusively, but to connote the more material side of our nature, which was formed, as we know, out of the dust of the earth. For the grain of truth in the matter, forced to such inappropriate and pretentious growth, lies not at all in the plays themselves, but in the primitive—and therefore

powerful, and admittedly most interesting—
stuff out of which they are moulded. But the
virtue of Shakespeare's work is that he took
this stuff, the crude story, or the murky legend
of blood feud and lust, and transmuted it into
spiritual tragedy. That has been plain enough
ever since his sources were known; and it is in
these, therefore, and even behind them again,
not in the plays, that the Freudian critic should
seek his quarry.

The artist's business is with spiritual tragedy.
What else, indeed, is tragedy but a reflection
of the struggle and suffering by which man's
spirit is enfranchised from the toils of the beast?
The scientist in his laboratory has another sort
of work to do; and man, when he gets him
there, is doubtless to be seen as quite another
sort of creature, a being far, far lower than the
angels. This is right. The scientist needs to
build his study upon facts which he can weigh
and measure, and the mortality common to all
men; and a fine square solid fortress of a building
he can erect, a refuge from many ills. But let him
not—I most humbly suggest—try to imprison
the spirit of man there, and range that among
his specimens; neither let the artist betray his
own ancient and honourable vocation by playing the jackal to such sacrilege.

It should be the producer's ideal also, once the production is planned and rehearsals are under way, to be this and no more. The more he can leave initiative to the actors the better. And, when he cannot, let him emulate the diplomat rather than the drill-sergeant, hint and coax and flatter and cajole, do anything rather than give orders; let them if possible still be persuaded that the initiative is theirs, not his. The Socratic method has its use, if there is time to employ it; an actor may be argued by it out of one way of thinking into another. But the immediate effect of this may be depressing, even paralysing —how his disciples must have loved Socrates to have been able to endure so much sweet reasonableness! The actor must then be heartened into starting afresh, and encouraged while he finds his way, and protected from the impatience of his fellow-actors, who have already found theirs. The production of a play—quite apart from the resultant performance—might be a most interesting business if it could be, as it should be, fairly adapted to every one of the diverse interests involved, if the finally needed unity were evolved from these and not imposed on them. But that is an ideal in larger matters than play producing—and remains one. Finally in this world, it would seem, someone has to give orders. But at least it need only be "finally", not "initially"; there is a practical middle course between anarchy and mere discipline—and play production can exemplify it, not inappositely. If a theatre existed in which dramatist-producer (in one person or two) and actors, self-disciplined to begin with, were used to setting to work together to realise the unity in diversity and diversity in unity, the freedom compatible with order, of a play's performance, it would be well worth the sociologist's while to study these means to that end. It would be worth Society's while to set up such a theatre—yes, for this most recondite reason only. "...to hold the mirror up to nature... "; but one may elaborate the simile. For in a play we see a section of Society itself, as we see in one of those convex mirrors an entire room arrestingly refracted. Of all the arts, drama, both in method and effect, can be the most exemplary.

But this is too high-falutin' talk for the theatre of to-day; for the producing of a play after three weeks' crowded rehearsals, with actors "swallowing" their words, the dramatist distressedly astonished to discover that these strange human beings are not in the least like the creatures of his imagination, the producer, surveying the blind struggle into existence, measuring the time to the fatal hour of performance, wondering when he must impose some sort of order, must put an end to the efforts to assimilate an understanding of the thing and say: Do it this way, whether you understand it or not. That roughly pictures what *is*; and the result is all that people know of dramatic art. Even the actors, comforted towards the last (and they need to be), and then, with luck, comforted again by generous applause, hardly dream of what might be. But—it is significant—what they will really have enjoyed is the rehearsing, even such wretchedly anxious rehearsing as this. If the play is a success, that is gratifying, of course. But note the loyalty of actors to a failure, when they feel that, given time, given one better chance or another, it need not have been a failure—since those rehearsals were so full of life and enjoyment. They are nearly always right. That was the play's true testing time. But how is anything in the least unusual to be put to the proof in three weeks' desperate rough-and-tumble? So the public tends to get "the mixture as before", and the actors to grow expert in nothing but administering it, and the popular theatre to be narrowly efficient; leaving perhaps nine-tenths of its potential wealth untouched, and two-thirds of its potential audience.

Page 28 (H) *This "lively study" will bring both sorts to life. But criticism will kill the first; and it will not kill the second sort.*

There is, of course, the play which depends upon the ingenuity of its plot; and the technique of this may be very interesting study, a necessary study, indeed, for those who mean to try their hands at playwriting. The rules of the "well made" play may one and all be transgressed—once you know what they are! But the relation of this technique to drama is the relation of prosody to poetry, and there is no need for such a means of studying it as we have been devising here. When I speak of plays, which criticism—applied to them even while they are thus being brought to life—will kill, I am thinking rather of those which may be full of fine poetry, clever ideas, striking characters; and yet...! Where is the flaw? Oftenest, I think, in the failure of the dramatist to eliminate *himself* from the play. How many people go to a play, sit through it and go home again, and never know the author's name! Well, that is

better than to have been unceasingly conscious
of the author, of *his* poetry, *his* ideas, *his*
characters. His credit should come later, when
we think the thing over—if he has given us
anything to think about. But that hour or so
of complete illusion, which is drama's peculiar
and triumphant gift to us, is only to be gained
by the dramatist's suppression of himself for
the time being in favour of his characters and
the actors of them. He must first create them
and then set them free.

Page 31 (I) ...*why should not this sort of a
theatre...be allowed to reckon its profits in
other terms than finance?*

I have never—I confess it in shame—been able
to find the argument to convince the "business
man" that a theatre should not necessarily
have to justify its artistic existence by "paying". There must be some such argument if one
could only find it; for, after all, business men
in France, Germany, Austria, Czecho-Slovakia,
Yugo-Slavia, Scandinavia (in Norway in the
days of her extremest poverty) were convinced
of this long ago. One can admit to him readily
enough that plays should not be produced to
empty houses, that a manager needs some cor-
roboration of his own judgment, and that the

public's money serves this purpose well enough. But from this he only argues that a play which costs £1000 to produce and brings in £750 is a bad play, that, at least, it should not be produced; whereas a play which costs £1000 to produce and brings in £1250 is a good play, and if it brings in £1500 it will be a better play, while if it costs £1000 to produce and brings in £5000 it must be a very good play indeed. Thus stated, the thing is absurd; but it is in effect what he is arguing when he tells me that a theatre devoted to good drama must justify its existence by being made to pay. If he said: I agree that, for such a theatre as this, popularity is no certain measure of a play's excellence and that one must do as many good plays as possible, that there is the taste of the minority to be considered, the mode of to-morrow to be developed, the tradition of the past to be preserved. On the other hand, the majority is not always wrong, a good play may be popular, or a popular play a good one— whichever way you like to put it—and even the theatre itself has a sort of right to find itself reasonably well furnished with spectators. Therefore, coming down to brass tacks, while our minimum income is so much, and so much more will be the maximum, we must budget accordingly; we must go to work economically, but we must see that the theatre's various dramatic interests are each fairly provided for. We ought, in fact, to draw up two budgets, one artistic and one financial, and then proceed to reconcile the two; *and I am prepared to admit that the financial, to be valid, must ensure the integrity of the artistic.* If this, or something like this, were the business-man's argument I think I could defend it against the most rabid apostle of art for art's sake. But I have never been able to get him so far. It is very strange. Nobody assumes for a moment that Opera can be made to pay. Opera, for some reason, fascinates the business man. In London, within the last fifty years, he must have flung something like a million pounds into it—the pampered public paying thirty shillings for a stall too! I have sometimes thought of advocating a theatre to be opened free gratis and for nothing, as the National Gallery is; but the business man would call that Communism. I wish that somebody who knows business men better than I do would find the right argument. For as I say, unless the English view of the drama as a simple trade is the only right view, and practically all other civilised countries are in the wrong, there must be one.

Page 38 (J) *Such variety as you do find...is superficial, a mask to the fundamental sameness of the fashionable thing.*

The ordinary playgoer does not realise the fundamental monotony—the *monotony in variety*—of the drama presented to him by the ordinary theatre. Thirty years ago the expert critic did not. But his point of view was that while these dramatic exercises by Ibsen, Maeterlinck, Tchekov, Shaw, Hauptmann, Strindberg, d'Annunzio might be interesting they were not plays. There were two reasons for this. The innately conservative French theatre was then the accepted modern standard; and Shakespeare, Sheridan and Goldsmith, the only old dramatists kept alive, were staged and had begun to be acted in as modern a fashion as possible. This, it was thought, was the way to keep them alive. Thirty years' experimenting in modern drama and its staging (some of this inevitably wild enough) and the cultivating of an historical sense of older dramatic methods have at least wrecked the basis of this barren complacency. The dramatist now ranges wide for his subjects, the producer is always after something new, and the critic, condemned to his stall for an average fifteen hours a week, is delighted to

64

welcome it. Yet a fundamental monotony pre-
vails. In what does it lie?

There is circumstantial monotony, so to call
it. In the Spanish drama of Echegaray's time,
nothing to count, it was said, would ever be
found in a first act, because the bulk of the
audience never turned up before the second.
The English theatrical historian of the future,
studying the daily papers, will discover that
from the time they began to go to press shortly
after midnight instead of at 3 a.m. the best plays
were those which began at 8.30 and ended sharp
at 11, and that most of these had short and
brisk last acts which added nothing new to their
story. The public will not come before 8.30;
and the critic of the morning paper, who has to
sit through the play both listening and making
up his mind what he is going to say about it,
will want to have his mind pretty well made up
by 10.30, and each minute after 11 which keeps
him from his taxi will be a mortal distress to
him. If he takes the job seriously his lot is really
a hard one, and that he should be able to write
anything but commonplace about commonplace
is a marvel. The dramatist, who is wise in his
generation, will do nothing to make it harder,
either by incontinently jerking the critical mind
from the groove into which it has settled, or

trying the critical temper by keeping that curtain up after the canonical hour has struck.

But it is a more pervasive and occult monotony which so wearies the ordinary adult-minded layman (who feels it no reproach to be ignorant of the latest play, actor, or production) that he can only endure a very occasional visit to the theatre. It is, with the average dramatist, the monotony of his way of approach to whatever the subject may be, and, with the actor, a consequent monotony of emotional appeal.

This emotional appeal is, of course, of the essence of the acted drama; it is incarnate in the very presence of the actor. And as it must be more or less spontaneously made, it is the harder to direct and control and diversify. There may be such a demand for it as we find in an Antony and Cleopatra or a Lear and Cordelia, characters full of meaning to be interpreted, beauty to be expressed, and calling besides for as much outpouring of emotion even in a single scene as might lay a strong man prostrate. Or it may need to be severely controlled, and refined into humour or deepened to meditation, as with an Alceste and a Célimène, a Rebecca West or Peer Gynt. Emotion surging out in the acting of such parts will only obscure their meaning; yet if it is absent they are lay

66

figures. Or the dramatist may merely give his actors a story told in dialogue by some skeletons of characters and leave them to do the rest, to fill out the emptiness with their personalities. They cannot add to the story unless they are to rewrite the dialogue. So to do their work— and the rest of the dramatist's—they are driven back, under one guise or another, upon emotional appeal.

It is moreover the easiest appeal to make and the surest of response, and an actor instinctively resorts to it when he finds that others are failing. If an audience is not held by an argument, is not smiling at the scene's wit, at the next opportunity charge your voice with manly emotion ("croon" a little; it is an admirable word), or, if you are a pretty girl, try that expressive droop of the eyelids (even though it expresses nothing in particular) and, ten chances to one, you will capture them again. I remember producing, a good many years ago, a play by Israel Zangwill called *The Revolted Daughter*. At one rehearsal, while Miss Nina Boucicault held forth very charmingly about women's rights (it was a topical play) to her handsome adorer, I noticed that he looked uncomfortable. So I asked him what was the matter. "Isn't this a little long?" he said. "Aren't you afraid

it'll bore them?" It was a little long, but I was
loyal to my author. "What I feel I ought to
do", he went on, "is just to take her in my arms
and kiss her." Zangwill was quite hurt; and,
needless to say, Miss Boucicault's revolt was
not brought to such a premature end. Now
possibly the actor was right, and the audience
did prove to be a little bored. What he did not
realise was that his simple remedy for their
boredom, though it might be effective for the
moment, was something more boring still, a
part of the perennial and cumulative boredom
of seeing the whole British drama dominated
by the certain threat that, whatever the problem of the play, it would sooner or later be
solved by some handsome gentleman taking
some desirable lady in his arms and kissing
her.

Things in this kind have improved; and
thanks, partly, to such pioneering as was *The
Revolted Daughter*, despite its little stretches of
dullness. The dramatist's horizon is certainly
wider than it was, and his characters are less
inevitably destined to be caught in "Cupid's
toils". The late Sir Harry Johnston was in some
ways a shockingly bad novelist, but he made
his books more interesting than most by their
simple assumption—natural to a man who had

68

been all his life in touch with realities, if incredible to the play-monger—that not more than, say, one-thirtieth of the normal man's time and energy is given to love-making, even when he is in love. And how better explain the vogue of the crime play and the history play (generically the same, it seems, but for costume) than by its comparative freedom from amorous obsession? For gangster and emperor must, to be recognisable, at least go through the motions of their trade. In the best crime play I remember it was not till three minutes to eleven that the hero, the amateur detective, asked the young woman whose innocence he had established whether she loved him. "Haven't you—", she answered, "haven't you known it all along?" *We* had, of course; and perhaps he had. But how grateful we had been to them both for their business-like self-restraint! The historical game is, of course, rather harder to play. Not every Napoleon at Wagram can stir us emotionally by his fighting of the battle with brain and will. And the ear-pinching and snuff-taking, the hand thrust into the waistcoat, the well-known straddle—by now he will have exhausted all these. So let him fetch out a miniature and press his lips to it unobserved. Thinking of Josephine; surely that ought to move us! And, since somehow he must move us, the temptation—both to dramatist and actor—is almost irresistible. It is one thing to take a subject; another, alack, to treat it and not shirk it.

This is the appeal surreptitious, of emotion degenerate into sentiment. It is the resource of a double charlatanism (none the less because the most distinguished practitioners employ it occasionally; but they do so with great discretion), the tricks of the actor reinforcing the tricks of the playwright; and it can secretly permeate and rot the very fabric of drama. The early nineteenth-century theatre of unbridled emotion died of an apoplexy, a theatre of sentiment will perish of pernicious anaemia. Its monotony is the monotony of the moribund. There has been in England since the war a sharp reaction against sentiment. Sob-stuff is now the refreshingly Spartan name for it. In the theatre its suavities have been replaced by a kind of Morse-code expressiveness, a dot-and-dash eloquence of brass clicks. But this is only to exchange one monotony for another, a dank for an arid one. And in art as in life—it is a commonplace—this fashionable toughness is at least as hollow as ever was old-fashioned sentiment. Moreover, while sentiment had, emotionally, no further to fall, toughness, when it does give way, will collapse into an hysterical welter of sob-stuff indeed.[1]

Clearly there is no salvation from monotony in variety of subject alone. What is wanted is

[1] A few weeks ago there appeared in the press a long letter written by one of the victims of a suicide pact. Her companion had killed himself first, and she had suffered agony, poor wretch—who could be so heartless as to doubt it?—as she watched his agonies. Nevertheless her description of them and of her later efforts to kill herself was—to the expert in such matters —sentiment at its crudest. Not only the expression of her feelings but the feelings themselves were borrowed from bad literature. She had dosed herself with them as with a drug. One could even discern that the dosing had begun long before, that the whole squalid business had been an intensifying succession of cheap heroics. Doubtless she believed in them, having nothing else so exciting to believe in. Did the man believe in them too, or had he simply not the heart or the moral courage to shame her by telling her it was all nonsense? Simpler to kill himself than to find a way out of the hysterical tangle! Did that dose of reality bring her for the moment to her senses? Her letter seems to show her flogging herself out of them again. The next thing was to drive her body to exhaustion; then (the final mental processes of the suicide are always obscure) she at last found courage to kill herself too.

wider resource in treatment, first from the dramatist, then from the actor. You may dress your performing dogs (I apologise for the simile) in a dozen different costumes, you may even exchange them for performing cats, but if they must everlastingly leap through the same hoops the most amenable of audiences will finally be bored. An opera may be full of good tunes, but if it is written throughout in the key of five flats and exclusively scored for the strings and the horns the least musical listeners will be wearied, though they may not know why. Neither dramatist nor actor to-day, in the every-day exercise of their calling, do more than adumbrate to us the rich resources of their art. Experimenting is difficult, I grant. If it is not to be costly, it must be done in a hole and a corner, and inadequate experiment is worse than useless. But it would be practical politics for the theatre to enlarge the field of its appeal; really to enlarge it, not merely pretend to by searching for fresh subjects and periods and costumes, and playing fresh tricks with them, while beneath it all there is only the same old play. So much that the theatre customarily did the cinema now does more entertainingly. If it can come to do nothing different the cinema may soon reduce it to a sort of economic—

ever an artistic—helotry. But if it will study
to discover and do what the cinema cannot hope
to (for one thing the cinema can never, I
think, acquire the theatre's peculiar *persuasive-
ness*) there is a larger audience being educated
for it by the cinema itself. The scene-painter, by
the way, has recently had a most costly experi-
mental fling. But the limits of what it is worth
while to do with inanimate paint and canvas,
even with the slightly more animate limelight,
are soon enough reached, and this seems to be,
for the moment, at an end. The limits to what
may be done with the literary medium of the
drama and the human medium of the actor are
in their very nature less calculable. I recall one
magnificent experiment (which we owed first to
Sean O'Casey, then to C. B. Cochran) in the
second act of *The Silver Tassie*. If its fine
symbolism had not been marred by a certain
pettiness it might have borne more fruit.
Clifford Bax adapted and staged a Socratic
dialogue, and there was astonished recognition
of its entertainment. Mr Bridie brought some
medical lore, ably handled, and a stimulating
brutality of treatment, to bear upon *A Sleeping
Clergyman*. There was the honest simplicity of
Richard of Bordeaux. And upon these two success waited. Dramatists, and actors too, are

ready enough to experiment, give them adequate means; that seems clear.[1]

But the task as a whole has this added difficulty; it involves the recruiting of an audience expert enough in the art of the drama to be alive to its possibilities, critically interested, not simply avid of sensation. We ourselves bring monotony to the theatre with the mood in which we commonly sit there; a lately dined, lazy-minded, passively sensuous mood. We look to be tickled under the one familiar rib. And if you who read and I who write are (we flatter ourselves) more critically alert than that, there will still be the fatuity of our neighbours; and to enjoy oneself in the theatre one must yield to the prevailing mood. "To be fair," says the professional critic, "I must own that the rest of the audience liked it." That betokens a more irritating evening for him than had the

---

[1] And as I correct these proofs there is published—only published!—a play, *St Helena*, by R. C. Sherriff and Jeanne de Casalis. It may have a touch too much of the monotony appropriate to its subject. But here is a Napoleon compassable by an actor (as most Napoleons are not; or should not be!). And the pleasure in seeing the play would be comparable to turning over a book of fine aquatints—living aquatints! Well, one does not complain that these are not Michelangelos.

whole theatre-full been bored. And to like a play when nobody else does is little better; we are then too conscious of the boredom of everyone around us to be able to enjoy it.

This sense of community in an audience is both a blessing and a curse to the drama. It can intensify enjoyment extraordinarily. The curse comes with the temptation to dramatist and actor to aim always at the thickest skull: if my shaft pierces that, you say, I am sure of the rest. But this is to forget—it has become the thing to ignore it in these days of combined mob-appeal and anti-democratic pose—that the levelling up of a common intelligence is as provedly feasible a feat as its levelling down. The process involves in the beginning, as does all learning, a certain amount of imitation, which may even be slightly spiced with hypocrisy; but one way of learning to like a thing is first to pretend that you do. Thereafter it may really be safely assumed that the best will be genuinely preferred to the worst—the best, that is to say, of its kind. And when it comes to a choice between kinds, the best of each kind are nearer akin than the best and the worst of one kind, and the way of liking between the two is easier to travel. If I appreciate Charlie Chaplin, and appreciate the difference between him and his imitators, I am the nearer to an appreciation of *King Lear* and the *Agamemnon*. It will only be the harder to please me, the merchants of entertainment may complain, since there is but one Charlie. Yes, it will be, if they have no more sense of their calling than a nose for the next best thing; and it had better be impossible to please on such terms. But I say that, for the honourably enterprising purveyor of drama, it is easier to please us if we are ready to be pleased with the best of *every* kind. I will even add, for his encouragement, of every semi-kind and demi-semi-kind, and of every fresh and competent *intention* in the way of drama that may be brought him. He need ask no wider scope.

The resources of drama are wide, and still largely unexplored. We have suffered a little in England (even while we have profited by them) from narrowly canalised "movements"; the Ibsen movement, the vogue for Shaw, Strindberg, Tchekov, for American efficiency, for German eclecticism. We have suffered because we have not had that critical taste for the drama in general, which would have let us put these things in their place and give to each its particular value. We accept the fashion of the moment, which peters out a moment later in imitation and monotony. Then we turn to the next fashion. The hope for the immediate future (as I say in my lecture) seems to lie in the widespread growth of a love and understanding of drama as drama. From that can perhaps be cultivated, with care and patience, something we can rightly call a taste for the art of the theatre. The present public appetite for it, though healthy enough, hardly deserves that name.

Page 43 (K) *For the Puritan prejudice, which once closed the theatres altogether, is by no means dead. It showed only the other day when...it prevented them, though it could not prevent the cinemas, from being opened on Sunday.*

The passing of "The Sunday Entertainments Bill" through Parliament was really the richest of comedies. About 1909 the cinemas, following the example of various concert societies, began to give Sunday performances "for charity". Renunciation of profit (and the giving away, perhaps, of a few free seats) let them evade, it was held, the consequences of the 1780 Sunday Observance Act, which would have been severe. The risk was worth taking, how-

77

ever; for "profit" is an elastic term, and their accountants saw to it that the cinemas did pretty well. Also it seemed a fairly safe risk; for the innovation was, needless to say, popular, and nobody in authority in England will meddle with the question of Sunday observance if he can help it. The London County Council, indeed, their chief Licensers, left them alone till 1916. And then a more or less covert bargain was made, that if the cinemas would behave nicely, and in particular see that their accountants took a rather more generous view of the profits due to charity, the Council would take no action. A sufficiently extraordinary bargain for a public authority to make; but the performances were very popular, the law was a little doubtful and the charities—the London Hospitals—now stood to benefit at the rate of about £100,000 a year. So everybody seemed to be happy; except the Lord's Day Observance Society and a few more such old-fashioned Puritans. But it was war time and Puritanism was at a discount. I take, by the way, the facts of the history from Lord Hailsham's speech in moving the second reading of the Bill in the House of Lords; I am sure he had them right. I now quote him verbatim.

"That practice continued for some fourteen

years, but in the year 1930 some other purveyors
of entertainment did not see why the cinemas
should enjoy this privileged position. By way
of registering their protest they initiated pro-
ceedings against the London County Council...
and it was held...that the...Council had no
right to exercise a dispensing power and to
excuse people who break the law. The result of
that was that all the Sunday performances were
declared to be illegal and anyone who had carried on one of them became liable to the penalty
prescribed by the Act of 1780."

Sunday concerts also could now be stopped;
it was even doubtful whether museums and
picture galleries would not have to be closed.
And there was £200 due to the Common In-
former (from, say, the Trustees of the British
Museum or the National Gallery) in respect of
each offence.

Plainly something had to be done. And the
"other purveyors of entertainment"—who were
the London theatre managers—reckoned that it
would be practically impossible to suppress the
Sunday cinemas, and equally impossible, to devise legislation, which should (particularly now
the "Talkies" had come in) permit the Sunday
performance of a play by mechanical means on
one side of a street and forbid its performance

by the same actors in their proper persons on the other. Yet this is what the Government and Parliament contrived to do.

The theatre managers had reckoned without the anomalous combination of forces which would be raised against them. There was, of course, Sabbatarianism itself, which fights every ditch in its lost battle, which appeals to principle but makes light of consistency, which (apparently) would see all England drunk on a Sunday afternoon for lack of other resort than the public-houses and use this as an excuse for closing them also. There was Labour, with its six-day-week gospel, a Sabbatarianism of self-protection, but just as crassly preached. There was the financial "pull" of the cinema companies, with their shareholders scattered over England, their dividends in danger if the Sunday privilege should be withdrawn. But how could they object to sharing the privilege with the theatres? They could not; though naturally they did not ask to. This was where the interests of the hospitals came in. Their £100,000 a year had been a sort of sanctified blackmail. Hard enough in any case to legalise the position and retain this forced payment of "profits" to charity; but, clearly, if every sort of entertainment were permitted the privilege would vanish, and with it all excuse for the levy. From this point of view alone, then, it was necessary to leave the theatres in the cold. One rash gentleman did protest in the House of Commons that if the Sabbath was to be desecrated it should be desecrated fairly; but Hansard reports that he was subjected to much interruption.

The political situation itself was against the theatres, and, indeed, against any careful legislation at all. The Labour Government had collapsed while a first Bill to remedy the trouble was still in the House of Commons. Then the National Government introduced a Bill, which it left to the free vote of the House; for Ministers themselves were divided in opinion, and as they had just had to sink their major political principles to keep the country going somehow they were the better pleased at the moment (those of them who were not worried half to death by more important problems) to exhibit principle upon such a minor matter as this. But this Bill collapsed, and an emergency Act re-establishing the *status quo ante* for a year had to be rushed through. Then the Government introduced a Bill to which they pledged themselves. It was, said Sir Herbert Samuel, in moving the second reading, "...undoubtedly illogical, but that need not disturb us too much, because most matters affecting this country are illogical, from the spelling of the English language down to the Constitution of the British Empire". But it was a practical Bill; which meant that it followed the line of least resistance, that Ministers' and Members' "principles" (as Sir Charles Oman obsolescently complained) might now be damned, and that with careful management and persistent "whipping" it could be manœuvred through—as it was!

In the debate on the second reading Sir Herbert Samuel and Mr Oliver Stanley contrived—though the challenge was explicit—to avoid mentioning the theatres altogether. That was masterly to begin with. But Mr Stanley's best work must have been done in Committee, where he had to meet definite amendments upon the theatre question. He brought his Bill triumphantly downstairs again with every one of them defeated; and on Report a final attempt, half-heartedly made, to put drama upon an equality with music and cinema was negatived without a division. Truly the debate had by then been much prolonged. The Government had seen to its starting with the discussion of a new clause for the setting up of a Film Institute, the decision being tactfully left to a free vote of the House; so Members, since they might upon this point be talking to some purpose, were encouraged to talk, and that took quite a time. Then came a question of a broken Ministerial pledge, of Mr Stanley's personal honour, with the usual explanations and apologies; and that took some time too. Then two or three Welsh members spoke at length of Wales's righteous desire to remain altogether uncontaminated by such a Bill, and quoted Welsh to the House—which must have been very interesting; and by that time, luckily, it was midnight and past. So when it came to the moving of the theatre amendment, and to a chance, upon the motion for a third reading, of reviewing the entire ridiculous position to which the Bill would bring Sunday entertainment for another generation or so, everybody was weary of the business, and the astute Mr Stanley could, in the fewest possible words, ask "...the House now to pass...a rather illogical and temporary Measure..."; and the House did. The "temporary", one supposes, was an excuse offered to his conscience; a quite illegitimate one, since there is nothing temporary about the Measure at all.

It should be added that during the Bill's progress a good deal (possibly a good many "deals" of one sort and another) must have been going on behind the scenes. The theatre folk were from the beginning divided among themselves—some of the actors fighting against the loss of their Sunday; and one sympathises with them—and, upon the eve of the third reading, even the militant Managers' Association had mysteriously climbed down.

It must also be said that Mr Stanley did not have any very remarkable debating force ranged against him. The more competent parliamentary hands will at once have grasped the governing facts of the situation; and why trouble to talk idly? Something had to be done; the cinema industry was an important one, much capital invested in it; the cinema-goers' votes were important. Because of that (the Government could argue) even the more Puritan malcontents would be secretly glad to vote for the Bill. Provide them with the excuse that this government of public safety would fall if they did not support it; and throw them, besides, the theatre, which commands neither capital nor votes, as a sacrifice to their righteousness, as something of a trophy—they would prove biddable enough.

Does the theatre really need or want to be allowed to open on Sundays? The commercial interests certainly want it; they are heavily handicapped by the deprivation. The actors would have to see that their six-day-week was preserved; but this Entertainments' Bill made that a provision for the cinemas. It may be mentioned that, if there were—as there should be—a few genuine repertory theatres in existence, the actors would risk no disadvantage here. Genuine repertory, in fact, gives the actor not six days' acting, but four or five— which can, besides, be genuine acting, not vain repetition, such as the heathen use. And if the public wants Sunday concerts and cinemas it obviously wants Sunday theatres too. It is a monstrous absurdity—even panic legislation has no right to inflict it—to allow a man to see a play in a cinema and forbid him to see it in a theatre. It is also likely that the average man would take to the theatre on his day of rest a fresher mind than he takes there on a working day. He might thus gradually come to prefer better drama to worse—and that would be something gained.

But what depresses one in the debates on the Sunday Entertainments Bill is not so much the ultimate result, nor even the occasional prejudice, silliness and vulgarity which throws into the shade such intelligence as was displayed (the two best considered speeches on the Bill as a whole were made—needless to say—in the House of Lords, by the Archbishop of Canterbury and Lord Snell), but the general failure to grasp the most salient point at issue. Mr Buchan and his supporters had half a hold on it in their pleadings for a Film Institute. Sir Charles Oman faced it, but did not seem to see it. For him "...the film industry as at present conducted is a deleterious agency corrupting the children of England..." and in default of any weekday salvation from this he would at least save them on Sundays from "Too hot for Paris" and "One mad kiss" by providing them with "Picturesque Palestine" or "Yak travel in Thibet" instead. One day's salvation in seven! And of such an efficiency! Really, he might arm his St Michael with sharper weapons than these. He may not, however, have been serious about the Yak travel. The humour in Hansard is sometimes hard to detect.

The point, surely, is this. Legislation may reasonably provide for the physical safety of the public in places of entertainment, may even limit the hours during which they shall be open. But the moment it touches the moral issue, whether of the nature of the entertainment itself or its suitability to a Sunday or a weekday, a merely prohibitory attitude becomes a futile, a barren, and finally a harmful one. It is the old question of the Censorship in a vaguer form. A Censorship is convenient; the sort of convenience that one adopts in war time and that short-sighted Governments continue in peace time. But it is a damming of the stream of thought; a dangerous thing to do. I wonder how much of the present licence in fiction, drama and film is not to be traced to the refusal of liberty to the dramatists of a generation ago, and the prejudices that prompted it. Censorship seems so practical; and it is not. You can prohibit certain overt offences, as you penalise burglary and murder. But Censorship and Sunday regulation will no more make entertainment wholesome and stimulating than the criminal law will in itself evoke a spirit of honesty and lovingkindness in a people. That needs positive encouragement. If it is agreed that in this matter Government must somehow concern itself with the moral issue, then it must be concerned with it positively and beneficently as well, or submit to seeing its prohibitory rules and regulations evaded and turned to ridicule or worse. Of what Censorship has that not been the lot?

The problem—whether it involves imaginative literature, or the drama, or any other sort of art—is admittedly not an easy one to tackle. For the moral issue at once becomes the aesthetic issue, and neither Governments nor Parliaments are apt to shine in dealing with that. And the aesthetic issue involves the propositions that it matters profoundly to a country whether its art is predominantly good or bad, and that good art is in itself a moral force; and to neither belief does British authority—its Puritan traditions for so long now debased by commercialism—show itself very ready to subscribe. Yet since this is a part of the general problem of educating the modern mass in that finer tradition of those old Humanities, which made the mind of the nation before ever harsh Puritanism hardened its heart; and since the present salvation of humanity itself may depend upon our finding a solution of that problem (for we race against time and evil competitors), it would be really worth the while of any Government to do something positive towards solving even this part of a part of it: how to enhance the quality of public entertainment?

Why should we think it any more of a problem or any more urgent to-day than it ever was? The answer is plain. The modern appeal to the enfranchised masses puts a premium upon whatever it asks no discrimination to enjoy. And modern taxation cuts off the margin of income with which the minority could and did provide themselves and their spiritual fellows with what was more to their taste. We are directly and indirectly taxing private patronage of the arts, of scholarship, and of research out of existence. We begin to see that we must put something effective in its place, till the time comes—if it is ever to come—when the masses will spontaneously demand the best of everything. But as to the arts—they are well enough in their way, one would sooner have them good than bad, but do they really matter? How many people in England honestly think so?

What to do for the benefit of public entertainment? When we have penalised such offences against public decency as can be agreed upon and definitely named, then trust no more in any Censorship, for weekdays or Sundays; but see that by one means or another there can be set in the balance against every poor play, cheap film, or worthless jumble of tunes, a good play, a good film, some good music, not of a single and superior kind, but each good of its own kind. *Then let the good and the bad fight it out.* And if the good is good surely it must win. This is not a quick way, but it is the only sure way by which a nation can be brought to prefer good art to bad. It answers, besides, to the present test of that freedom under government (the two in equilibrium) by which England agrees to go her ways in general.

Government is not asked, needless to say, directly to provide good entertainment for the people. One has not even to plead the particular cause of National Theatre or Opera. There are a variety of ways by which the thing can be done; and variety will in itself be best. What is important is to see the situation as it is to-day, not as it used to be once upon a time, and to admit that positive action is needed. And when Mr Oliver Stanley tells the House of Commons that it has really spent too much time over the Sunday entertainment question, one is disposed to retort: Yes, and the time it did spend was, from any statesmanlike point of view, mainly wasted.

When the theatre managers feel that revenge is due to them for that scurvy measure they might do worse than stage a dramatic version of the debates on it, as a comic Sunday entertainment—and no money need be taken at the doors! Some compression would be advisable. But one could, in fairness, give more place to the "serious interest" than the Government felt it wise to do—when they saw their chance, under cover of the general shindy, at least to free picture galleries and museums and concerts from any future badgering by the Lord's Day Observance Society. For that at least they are to be thanked. One would also emphasise the precedent created by the 5 per cent. tax on cinemas for the support of a Cinema Institute (*I* should, at any rate; but I fear the theatre managers might not wish to). Why not a 5 per cent. tax for the support of a National Theatre, which would be a National School of the Theatre both for actors and public? One might even elaborate a little—but it would be un-kind—the Solicitor-General's artless reply to the accusation that this was an unprincipled measure: " . . . It is a cardinal principle of this Bill with regard to cinemas to reproduce the *status quo* ". Which, being practically applied, can only mean that if you succeed in defying the law for ten years or so the principles of government demand that your defiance shall be legalised. Strange doctrine from a Law Officer of the Crown ! Yes, one could make both an amusing and instructive Sunday entertain-ment out of the debates on the Sunday Enter-tainments Bill.

But it is ill gibing at politicians because they cannot afford to be statesmen all the time. The Government were in a hole and had to get out of it somehow, and, to do them justice, they made no bones about that. But when the more guilty among the Ministers are less harassed, when next they are in Opposition perhaps, they might give a few minutes thought to the true issue involved, which their legislative botching did so little to clarify, so much to obscure.

Page 44 (L) *The theatre, in any case, has to be organised: it is the one art which cannot escape it. I do not doubt that its turn will come.*

Have the Society for bringing foreign tourists to England, the Railways, Steamship Companies, Hotel-keepers and the other interests involved, ever considered what the attraction would be of *one really first-class theatre* in London, a theatre *fully* representative of English drama, the classic and the modern, *at its best*? Even Stratford-on-Avon attracts thousands yearly. Americans in tens of thousands used to go to Germany to study the drama there, many to Copenhagen also; and those that had the time and the money would go on to Russia. Germany has now, for the moment, knocked its drama on the head. Russia can hardly attract tourists. The French theatre is in the trough of a wave, the Italian in a yet worse case. England has better material of this kind than any country in Europe. Even from a commercial point of view it would pay her to organise and use it. But let us be clear that what is wanted is not a mere place of amusement. People do not make pilgrimages to be amused. But they do still make them, some to Lourdes and to Rome, to Mecca and Benares, others to the shrines of art and learning, for the salvation of their souls. It is vexing to see a country's wealth left unemployed. It is hard to be patient with that peculiarly British form of snobbery, the refusal to take art seriously because certain pretentious bores take it solemnly, the mock-modest cant of the proclaimed lowbrow. And if you really are stupid, it is surely better not to boast about it.

www.ingramcontent.com/pod-product-compliance
Ingram Content Group UK Ltd.
Pitfield, Milton Keynes, MK11 3LW, UK
UKHW042147280225
455719UK00001B/162